52 WEEKS OF Family SPANISH

Bite Sized Weekly Lessons
Designed to Get You and Your
Family Speaking

SPANISH TODAY!

BY: EILEEN MC AREE

52 Weeks of Family Spanish
Text Copyright 2016 Eileen Mc Aree

Dedication

This book is dedicated to Marguerite, Eva, James and Rose. Thanks for being my test subjects, fellow classmates and biggest cheerleaders. Los quiero.

Contents

Author's Note: 7

Introduction 9

How to Use This Book..11

Suggested Activities 13

Pronunciation Guide...17

Words and Phrases to Get You Started................................20

A Little Monthly Wisdom..25

52 Week Curriculum...29

Unit 1: Making Friends...31

    Week 1: Manners 32

    Week 2: Greetings..33

    Week 3: Introductions..34

    Week 4: What's Your Name?..35

    Week 5: How Old Are You? 36

    Week 6: More Greetings 38

    Week 7: Nice to Meet You! 39

    Week 8: Review..40

Unit 2: All About Me 41

    Week 9: Who Am I? 42

    Week 10: Feelings..43

    Week 11: What Do I Look Like?..44

    Week 12: What Do I Look Like?..46

    Week 13: What I Like to Do..48

    Week 14: My Face 49

    Week 15: My Body 51

    Week 16: Review..52

Unit 3: Welcome to My Home 53

    Week 17: Welcome to My Home 54

    Week 18: Where Is It?..55

    Week 19: Where Is _____? 56

    Week 20: Meet My Family (A)...57

    Week 21: Meet My Family (B)...58

    Week 22: Meet My Family (C)...59

    Week 23: His Name Is_____.....................................61

    Week 24: Review..62

Unit 4: Useful Information 63

   Week 25: Days of the Week 64

   Week 26: What Day is Today? 66

   Week 27:Numbers 1-10 67

   Week 28: How Many? 69

   Week 29: Months 70

   Week 30: I know 72

   Week 31: When Is Your Birthday? 73

   Week 32: Review 74

Unit 5: Mealtimes 75

   Week 33: I'm Hungry 76

   Week 34: Favorite Foods 77

   Week 35: I Like 78

   Week 36: I'm Thirsty! 79

   Week 37: Can I have......? 80

   Week 38: Sit at the Table 81

   Week 39: Where is my.....? 82

   Week 40: Review 83

Unit 6: Getting Ready 85

   Week 41: Wake Up! 86

   Week 42: Getting Ready 87

   Week 43: I want to wear.....(A) 88

   Week 44: I want to wear ...(B) 89

   Week 45: Where are your shoes? 91

   Week 46: It's time to go! 92

   Week 47: Have a good day! 93

   Week 48: Review 94

Unit 7: A Few Odds and Ends 95

   Week 49: Things Around the House 96

   Week 50: Things in Our World. 97

   Week 51: Places We Go 99

   Week 52: Review 100

Where Do I Go From Here? 101

Learning Resources 103

Glossary of Terms 109

About Author 121

Author's Note:

It has been quite a few years since my family and I started our Spanish learning adventure. In the beginning, I was a stay at home mother with a houseful of preschoolers, toddlers and an infant. I thought I would brush up on my high school Spanish as a way to make myself more marketable for when it was time to reenter the workforce. Additionally, I could enrich my chidren's lives with a second language! The idea for this book was born when I realized how difficult it was to stick with a "program". In the midst of diaper changes, laundry and general child raising, formal teaching of a language that was foreign to both me and my children was difficult to find time for. Instead, I would introduce a little at a time, and make a game of it. I knew from my experience as a teacher that a little practice goes a long way.

So....did it work? Was I successful? Do my children speak Spanish?

Well, that depends on your definition of success. When I started this process I had a very different idea of what success would mean. I did not have a clear picture of just how much language (or how little, depending on how you look at it) you need to communicate in a second language. Luckily for me, I discovered a passion when I started studying Spanish. It's a hobby for me: something I enjoy spending time at, cultivating and sharing with my children. That in itself could be considered a win. However, to be more definitive, here is what I learned over the past six years while studying and teaching Spanish:

1. I speak Spanish. Yes, I do! I can converse with native speakers in clear, if sometimes halting Spanish. I can read Spanish. I can understand about 80% of what I hear on the radio. Periodically I discover my Spanish has "jumped" and all of a sudden I can understand more than I could a few months ago. It is exciting and rewarding.

2. My children have a basic understanding of Spanish. They know more Spanish than they would have had I depended on school or an enrichment program to teach them. These competencies include:

- The ability (and willingness) to exchange basic pleasantries in a foreign language

- The ability to make basic requests in Spanish (they have to in order to get their hands on their Ipods!)

- An understanding of gender agreement, conjugation and number agreement.

- A good accent and the understanding that you have to pronounce words in a foreign language according to the rules of that language or you are speaking incorrectly

- A growing vocabulary.

- An interest in foreign language and culture

- Friends! I needed to speak Spanish in order to improve. In the course of this, I was lucky to make friends with other mothers from Mexico, Ecuador and El Salvador. Although all our children speak English together, it was wonderful to meet some new families with different cultures and traditions.

So... is that success? I think so. I am sure my children would speak more Spanish if I had the discipline to run an organized Spanish program. Unfortunately, although we are no longer changing diapers and cleaning sippy cups at our home, the challenges of school, sports, chores and other obligations have kept us learning Spanish one week at a time. We have learned that acquiring a second language is not a race to the finish line, but a path toward a continuously moving target. I am happy to report that my children love foreign language in general. My two oldest take French at school (of course!) and are already asking for exchange student trips. Somewhere in the midst of all this chaos there is another 52 Weeks of More Family Spanish cooking, but for now I earnestly hope this book encourages you to view language learning as an attainable, worthwhile goal.

Buena suerte!   *Good luck!*

bwehn-ah swayr-tay

Introduction

Learning a foreign language is a wonderful goal, and it can also be a fun and rewarding experience. What stops many people from attempting to learn a foreign language is their own fear of speaking, of looking foolish in front of another person. They may be comfortable studying vocabulary lists or grammar rules, but without actually speaking a language, no one can really progress. 52 Weeks of Family Spanish is designed to get you speaking Spanish from the very first day!

Not only will you build on your own success as you learn to communicate in Spanish, you will take your children along on this exciting journey. Children are naturally curious and full of enthusiasm. They haven't yet faced a conjugated verb or a double negative. They have no idea that learning to speak a foreign language is supposed to be difficult. What better study partners could you ask for? For most of us, our inhibitions about pronouncing foreign words disappear when we practice with our children. Using the simple lessons provided in this book, you and your children will be speaking to each other (and hopefully other people) in Spanish quickly and easily.

52 Weeks of Family Spanish is designed to be a relaxed, self- teaching guide. Each week you focus on a simple conversational concept that you and your children can practice together. The conversations were chosen based on their relevance to real, everyday family life. The lessons are short and simple and will get you and your family practicing Spanish in the many of the moments modern families share together: mealtimes, morning "rush hour", carpools, bedtime. This is an oral introduction to the Spanish language, so there are no spelling rules to memorize or flashcards to flip. Grammar is touched on throughout the curriculum but the main goal is to get you and your family speaking this beautiful language.

FEATURES OF THE BOOK

Before you begin, take a look through the book. There are several features that will make the learning process easier for both you and your children.

- ## Words and Phrases to Get You Started

  These is a small compilation of some words and phrases you should know from the beginning to encourage and instruct your children.

- ## Pronunciation Guide

  This is a simple, easy to understand guide to the sounds of the Spanish language.

- ## 52 Week Curriculum

  This is the heart of it all, and when you see how simple each week's lesson is, you may be surprised. Certain weeks focus on only one phrase! The fact is that fifty-two small, achievable lessons add up to quite a store of conversational skills, and conversation is the ultimate goal of this book. It was written to provide a family with a respectable oral vocabulary in about a year. Exactly how fast your family progresses is entirely up to you. If you and your kids are in a groove and you want to move ahead, by all means follow the momentum. On the other hand, if you are dealing with an ear infection, an impending dance recital and a huge deadline at work, stretch one week's lesson into three weeks. The pace is yours to decide. You and your family will be successful if you simply *keep talking*.

- ## Suggested Activities

  As every busy parent knows, it is not always easy to find time to go to the supermarket, let alone learn *and teach* a brand new language. This section is full of realistic, fun and engaging ways to practice your Spanish skills in the context of your everyday life.

- ## Resources

  Listed here are many wonderful materials available to make learning a foreign language fun and engaging. The internet makes it possible to access many educational games for free. For those with "smart" phones, there are apps that can reinforce language learning while you wait outside school, in a fast food pick up line, or entertain a younger sibling at baseball practice. Also listed here are some books and CD's that can further pique your child's interest in the Spanish language.

How to Use This Book

1. 52 WEEKS OF FAMILY SPANISH follows an auditory and oral learning model. Listening to the sounds of a new language and communicating successfully in that language opens the mind to a new structure of thinking. Vocabulary drills and grammar rules shut down the learning process at this early stage. This is not to imply vocabulary and grammar are not crucial to the mastery of any language. It is simply that to get the process started, the natural way is to start talking.

2. TALK, TALK, TALK! Use your new vocabulary every day, even it is only for a one minute conversation. You will be surprised and pleased to see how a minimal time commitment, every day, leads to the attainment of a great deal of vocabulary.

3. WATCH YOUR PRONUNCIATION. Try to correct any major pronunciation errors as soon as they occur. The pronunciation guides should help you with this. The faster you correct yourself, the faster you will learn.

4. TOUCH ON EACH WEEK'S CULTURAL NOTE. Every week's lesson includes a fact about a country or culture where Spanish is spoken. Introducing children to different Latin cultures increases their curiosity about the language. It makes the process more interesting and fun for you as well!

5. TAKE TIME TO REVIEW. Review weeks are built into the curriculum. Take your time! If you feel you and your family haven't mastered one week's concept, continue your review till you are ready to move on.

6. REMEMBER, IT'S A JOURNEY, not a race. Many language courses advertise mastery of a language in record time. Babies don't learn to talk overnight, and people don't speak new languages overnight either. Your Spanish speaking skills will continue to improve as long as you keep speaking and learning. Enjoy!

Suggested Activities

1. **Short and sweet conversations.** Each week's lesson is bite size Spanish concept that you can review during a five minute conversation. Resist the impulse to drill, if your child forgot a word, just provide it for them. The repetition of language will help their vocabulary grow. Great places for bite-sized conversations are:

    *   In the car...all parents spend plenty of time in the car! Use this time to squeeze in some language learning.

    *   At mealtimes...many of the lessons in this book are perfect to review before breakfast, lunch or dinner...or snack at the pool...or a snack in the mall.....

    *   Bedtimes...start with "Te quiero" and move on from there!

    *   "Downtime"...Waiting in the pediatrician's examination room, waiting for your food to be delivered at Chili's, anytime or place you need to kill five minutes, use it to review Spanish!

2. Put on the radio. By putting on Spanish language radio in the car or kitchen while you make dinner, you acclimate your ear, and your children's if they are listening, to the rhythm and cadence of Spanish speech. You are hearing native or fluent speakers provide an accent model as well.

3. Find a Spanish language children's TV show. A TV show provides all the benefits of listening to a radio program with the additional visual component. Children's television shows are not terribly complicated in terms of character and plot, and you can derive meaning just by watching. Your child will be delighted with himself when he hears a word he understands or can follow the storyline on his own.

4. Read a bilingual storybook. Most local libraries have a great selection of children's picture books in both English and Spanish. The plots are simple so you can get a lot of meaning from the picture clues. Also, reading aloud to your children helps you work on your accent.

5. Say hello! One of the hardest parts of learning a new language is overcoming our own embarrassment and communicating with native speakers. If you can get over this hurdle you will have conquered a challenge that turns many people away from learning a second language. Put yourself out there and wish, "Buenos días", to the Peruvian shopkeeper in your town. Exchange pleasantries in Spanish with a mom at the local playground. Encourage your children to do the same.

6. Make friends. One of the benefits of being friendly to your Spanish speaking neighbors is the opportunity to meet new, interesting people and make new friends. This is even easier for your children. There are many places for children to meet and play with children who speak Spanish. Local libraries, playgrounds, library story hours and community pools are all good examples. Typically, children in the United States will speak English, but if you chat away to the moms or dads your kids may begin to chat in Spanish as well. People are usually friendly. Oftentimes, these hybrid Spanish-English conversations will be very helpful to you and may provide some useful practice for the person with which you are speaking.

7. Start a playgroup. If you don't feel brave enough to approach a total stranger, consider trying a more formal social setting. Most communities offer bilingual story hours or playgroups. Another option is to start your own playgroup. You can invite native speakers trying to learn English, or other parents practicing Spanish, whatever you feel comfortable with. Internet sites like Meetup. com are great tools for creating playgroups.

8. Play. Have fun with Spanish. The Resources section lists lots of fun games, books and CD's to support your learning. In addition, try playing the following vocabulary review games with your kids:

- ¿Dónde Está? Ask your children where different items in the room are. They recognize the vocabulary word and point to the item.

- ¿Caliente o Frío? This is your basic game of hot or cold except instead of hiding an object in the room, you think of an item in the room. You then direct your children toward it with cues of caliente o frío. The child who figures out which item you were thinking of (lamp, television, etc.) must call out the name of the item in Spanish.

- Mamá (Papá) Dice, "Toca tu..." Here is a version of Simon says. Mommy (or Daddy) says to touch different body parts, items in the room, items of clothing etc. Children must understand the vocabulary they are hearing in order to act accordingly. They are out if they touch something and Mama didn't say!

- Veinte Preguntas. Children are given the opportunity to ask twenty questions to figure out the item you are thinking of. They can ask questions about it in English (or Spanish as their knowledge increases) but they have to guess what it is in Spanish.

- Yo Veo Algo….. Play this game the same way you would play I Spy. As your vocabulary increases you can use more and more Spanish describing words to help your children puzzle out what you see.

- Puppets. Puppets are an invaluable tool for teaching language. Buy or make a hand puppet, name your puppet (I favored Spanish names to go with our theme!), and make the puppet your Spanish teacher's helper. Anytime you want to review dialog, take out your puppet and talk away. Older children can help put on the puppet show for younger children.

- Beanbag Toss. This is simply another way to review vocabulary. Get a beanbag (or soft, small ball, or stuffed animal, anything that won't go through a window or cause a concussion). The first person says a word or phrase in Spanish and tosses the beanbag to the next person who then has to give the translation. If they don't get the correct answer, they are out. If they do get the correct answer, they come up with another Spanish phrase and toss the beanbag to the next person. You can reverse this activity and say the words or phrases in English and have the children provide the Spanish translation. That is always a little harder!

Pronunciation Guide

An informal pronunciation key is provided beside each word or phrase provided in this book. A look below will give you an idea of general pronunciation of the Spanish language. Remember: there are differences in pronunciation in the Spanish spoken in different regions of the world. The information below is a general guide to South American Spanish.

One of the nicest surprises about learning Spanish is discovering how uniform their sound system is. Unlike the tricky English language, Spanish is spoken the way it is written, and each letter or letter combination generally has one singular sound. Once you learn it properly, you will be able to pronounce longer and more complicated phrases with ease. The whole point of this book is to try and help the beginning learner get over their fear of appearing foolish when speaking a new language. Practice your pronunciation with your children, but remember: when you gather your courage to speak Spanish to a native speaker they will NOT laugh if your pronunciation is a little off. As a matter of fact, as long as they can generally understand what you are trying to say, most people won't even comment if you mispronounce a word. Would you? Use this guide to get you started, and then as you listen to authentic Spanish accents you will perfect your pronunciation through imitation.

VOWELS

CORRECT PRONUNCIATION OF THE VOWEL SOUNDS IS THE KEY TO BEING UNDERSTOOD. REMEMBER: YOU WILL PRONOUNCE THE VOWEL THE SAME WAY EACH TIME. SIMPLE!

Letter	Pronunciation	Spanish Examples
a	like a in father	cama (kah-mah)
e	like a in late	de (day)
i	like ee in feet	sí (see)
o	like o in rope	solo (soh-loh)
u	like oo in loot	usar (oos-ahr)
y	like ee in feet	y (ee)

VOWEL COMBINATIONS

ie	sounds like y in yes	bien (byehn)
ua	w like in wind	aqua(ah- gwah)
ue		buen (bwayn)
ui		huir (hweer)

CONSONANTS

ch, f, k, l, m, n, p, t, y c, s	generally as in English	
b and v	generally pronounced like an English b. When placed between vowels, more like a combination of b and v, a little softer than an English b	bamba (bahm-ba) vamos (bah-mohs) labio (lah-bee-yoh)

d	generally similar to English d, but with the tip of the tongue against the top row of teeth. Try for a sound between a d and th.	dónde(dohn-day) vida (bee-dah)
g	before i and e sounds like the English h. Otherwise, pronounced as in English	gente (hen-tay) gustar (goo-star)
h	silent	hasta (ahs-tah)
j	spoken like the English h	joven (ho-ben)
ll	most commonly pronounced like y	lleno (yay-noh)
ñ	sounds like ni in onion	año (ah-nyoh)
qu	spoken like English k	que (kay)
r	*trilled, especially at start of word	aroma (ah-roh-mah)
rr	*strongly trilled	arroz (ah- rrohs)

*YOU HAVE TO LISTEN TO A TRILLED R TO UNDERSTAND THE SOUND. YOU WILL RECOGNIZE IT AND PRODUCE A TRILLED R WITH TIME AND PRACTICE.

x	usually pronounced as in English, but before a consonant the sound changes to s	examen (eks-ahm-ehn) extrano (ehs-trah-nyoh)
z	sounds like English s	brazo (brah-soh)

Words and Phrases to Get You Started

As an individual, you are embarking on a journey to learn Spanish. As a parent, you are additionally taking on the role of teacher. With this knowledge in mind, prepare yourself from day one with some basic vocabulary that will guide and encourage your children. It also adds to the language they will pick up through exposure!

Please note: This is a beginner's guide. Rather than presenting all commands in various tenses and persons, for the sake of simplicity, all commands here are presented in the singular informal. If you were commanding all of your children at once, you would conjugate the verbs differently. For now, use this simple form and hope that when you tell one of your children to do something they infer that you want them all to do the same!

Imperativos: Commands:

ihm-payr-ah-tee-bohs

ven aquí   come here
behn-ah-kee

tranquila   calm down
trahn-kee-lah

escucha   listen
ehs-koo-chah

sietate   sit down
see-yeh-tah-tay

oye   Look out!
oh-yay

dimelo dee-may-loh	say it to me
abre ah-bray	open
cierra see-yair-ah	close
Comparte kohm-pahr-tay	share
Compórtate bien kohm-pohr-tah-tay bee-yehn	behave yourself
Damelo dah-may-loh	give it to me
Para pah-rah	stop
Ten cuidado tehn kwee-dah-doh	Be careful
Intenta una vez más: In-tehn-tah oon-ah vays mahs	Try again.
Dime otra vez: dee-may oh-trah bays	Tell me again.
Repita, por favor: reh-pee-tah pohr fah-bohr	Repeat, please.

Pedidos:

peh-dee-dohs

Puedo tener...
pway-doh tehn-air

Necesito mas
neh-seh-see-toh mahs

Ayudame, por favor
ah-yoo-dah-may pohr fah-bohr

Quisiera...
kee-see-yair-ah

Me gustaría...
may goos-tah-ree-yah

Requests:

Can I have..

I need more..

Please help me.

I want... (this is a more
polite way of saying "I want")

I would like...

Elegios:

eh-leh -hee-yohs

¡Muy bien!:
mooy byehn

¡Fantástico!:
fahn-tahs-tee-koh

¡Maravilloso!:
mahr-ah-bee-yoh-soh

¡Qué bonita!
kay-boh-nee-tah

Praise:

Very good!

Fantastic!

Marvellous!

How pretty!

Qué bien!: kay byehn	How nice.
¡Buen trabajo!: bwehn trah-bah-hoh	Good job!
⬚Así es! ah-see ehs	That's it!
⬚Perfecto! payr-fehk-toh	Perfect!
Y sobre todo… ee-soh-bray-toh-doh	And most importantly…
Lo quiero! loh kee-yair-oh	I love you!
Mi amor mee ahm-ohr	My love
Mi vida mee-bee-dah	my life
Mi angelito/a mee ahn-hehl-lee-toh/tah	My angel
Nena/e nay-nah/nay	cute little girl or boy
Cariño/a kah-ree-nyoh/ah	Sweetie

Dulzera/o	Honey
dool-sair-ah/oh	
Mi querida/o	My darling
mee kay-ree-dah/oh	
Mi Corazon	My sweetheart
mee koh-rah-zohn	

A Little Monthly Wisdom

In order to increase the Spanish communication in your home, add some traditional Spanish proverbs to your parenting toolbox. Here are twelve proverbs from all over the Spanish speaking world. You can adopt one a month, to both help you with your pronunciation as well as assist your children with their listening comprehension. The proverbs were chosen for their versatility toward a plethora of common family situations: sibling arguments, chore completion, homework encouragement, etc.

1. A QUIÉN MADRUGA, DIOS LE AYUDA.

*ah-kee-**yehn** mah-**droo**-gah, **dee**-ohs lay ah-**yoo**-dah*

Literal translation: He who rises early, God helps.

English equivalent: The early bird gets the worm

2. DONDE HAY GANA, HAY MAÑA.

dohn-day eye gah-nah, eye mah-nyah

Literal translation: Where there is the desire there is the ability.

English equivalent: Where there is a will, there is a way.

3. POCO A POCO SE ANDA LEJOS.

poh-koh ah poh-koh say ahn-dah lay-hohs

Literal translation: Little by little one goes far.

English translation: Put one foot in front of the other, keep at it!

4. LO PASADO, PASADO ESTÁ.

loh pah-sah-dah, pah-sah-dah ehs-tah

Literal Translation:. It past, the past it is.

English equivalent: Let it go; let bygones be bygones, the past is in the past.

5. UN MAL TIEMPO, BUENA CARA.

oon mahl tee-yehn-poh, bwehn ah cah-rah

Literal translation: In bad times, put on a good face.

English equivalent: Look on the bright side.

6. DONDE COMEN DOS, COMEN TRES.

dohn-day koh-mehn dohs, koh-mehn trays
Literal translation:

Wherever two people eat, three people eat.

English translation: There's always room for one more.

7. EL MEJOR ESCRIBANO ECHA UN BORRÓN.

ehl may-hohr ehs-scree-bah=noh eh-chah oon bohr-rohn

Literal translation: The best scribe makes a blot.

English equivalent: Everybody makes mistakes.

8.CUANDO HAY HAMBRE, NO HAY MAL PAN

kwahn-doh eye ahm-bray, no eye mahl pahn

Literal translation: When there is hunger, there is no bad bread

English equivalent: Hunger makes good sauce!

9.ALGO ES ALGO; MENOS ES NADA.

ahl-goh ehs ahl-goh, may-nohs ehs nah-dah

Literal translation: Something is something; less is nothing.

English equivalent: It's better than nothing!

10.UN VIAJE DE MUCHAS MILLAS EMPIEZA CON UN PASO.

oon bee-yah-hay day moo-chahs mee-yahs ehm-pee-yay-sah cohn oon pah-soh

Literal translation: A trip of a thousand miles begins with a single step.

English equivalent: You have to start somewhere.

11.ASÍ ES LA VIDA

ah-see ehs lah bee-dah

Literal translation: So is life!

English equivalent: That's life! Deal with it!

12. EL TRABAJO COMPARTIDO ES MAS LLEVADERO

ehl trah-bah-hoh cohm-pahr-tee-doh ehs mahs yay-bah-dayr-oh

Literal translation: Shared work is more bearable.

English equivalent: Many hands make light work.

52 Week Curriculum

Here is an overview of how the weeks of your year of learning Spanish are divided. Topics were chosen for ease of learning and application to real life. Suggested reviews are included in each week's lesson. Don't feel compelled to go in order! If you want to learn how to say, "I'm hungry!" in Spanish, by all means skip straight to Unit 5. Remember, go in an order that is interesting to you and at a speed you and your family are comfortable with. This book was written to make Spanish learning easy and fun!

UNIT 1: WEEKS 1-8

THEME: MAKING FRIENDS

CULTURAL SPOTLIGHT: MEXICO

UNIT 2: WEEKS 9-16

THEME: ALL ABOUT ME

CULTURAL HIGHLIGHT: SPAIN

UNIT 3: WEEKS 17-24

THEME: WELCOME TO MY HOME

CULTURAL SPOTLIGHT: HONDURAS

UNIT 4: WEEKS 25-32

THEME: USEFUL INFORMATION

CULTURAL SPOTLIGHT: ARGENTINA

UNIT 5: WEEKS 33-40

THEME: MEALTIMES

CULTURAL SPOTLIGHT: PUERTO RICO

UNIT 6: 41-48

THEME: GETTING READY

CULTURAL SPOTLIGHT: SPANISH INFLUENCE IN THE UNITED STATES

UNIT 7: WEEKS 49-52

THEME: A FEW ODDS AND ENDS

CULTURAL SPOTLIGHT: SPANISH LANGUAGE AROUND THE WORLD

Unit 1:
Making Friends

Week 1: Manners

Vocabulary: sí/no   (yes/no)
see/noh

por favor   (please)
pohr fah-bohr

gracias   (thanks)
grah-see-ahs

muchas gracias   (thank you very much)
moo-chahs grah-see-ahs

de nada   (you're welcome)
day-nah-dah

Pronunciation note: Listen to a Spanish r. It sounds very different from an English r. Try to trill your r. Practice! It's fun!

Cultural Note: Mexico is our neighbor to the south. Popular breakfast dishes are huevos rancheros, which is like scrambled eggs, tortillas with beans or tortillas stuffed with beef or chicken.

Idea! Use your new manners words at mealtimes. Pair the English word of whatever you want with the Spanish manners word. Encourage your children to do the same. Don't worry about mixing up the languages, that's how communication is born.

Week 2: Greetings

Review: Week 1: Manners

Vocabulary:

Hola	(hello)
oh-lah	
Adiós	(goodbye)
ah-dee-ohs	
Buenos días	(Good morning)
bwehn-ohs-dee-ahs	
Buenas tardes	(Good afternoon)
bwehn-ahs-tahr-days	
Buenas noches	(Good evening)
bwehn-ahs-noh-chays	

Pronunciation note: The letter h is silent in Spanish.

Cultural Note: Mexican children love to play sports just like children in the United States. They play soccer, which in Mexico, and many other parts of the world, is called football. They also play baseball and a game called jai alai high-uh-ligh.

Idea! Try greeting some friends or family members with a friendly, "¡Hola!".

Week 3: Introductions

Review: Week 2: Greetings

Vocabulary: ¿Cómo estás?   How are you?
koh-moh ehs-tah

bien   good
bee-ehn

mal   bad
mahl

muy   very
moy

¿Y tú?   and you?
ee too

Grammar note: The phrase, "¿y tú?" is a way of returning the question, "How are you?". In English we would say, "Fine, thanks. How are you?". Spanish is the same. It is a pleasantry.

Cultural Note: There are more Spanish speakers in Mexico than in Spain!

Idea! Have fun role playing out a simple conversation with your children. Kids can respond that they are well:

Hola!¿ Cómo estás?   Bien! ¿Y tú?
Bien, gracias.   or not so well:
¡Hola! ¿Cómo estás?   Muy mal! ¿Y tú?
Bien. ¡Adiós!

ENCOURAGE YOUR CHILDREN TO HAM IT UP!

Week 4: What's Your Name?

Review: Week 2: Greetings

Vocabulary: ¿ Cómo te llamas?   What's your name?

koh-moh tay-yah-mahs

Me llamo_____.   My name is_____.

may yah-moh

Pronunciation note: In Spanish, ll is its own special sound. It most Spanish speaking parts of the word it is pronounced like the English y.

Cultural note: Hundreds of years ago, people called the Aztec lived in Mexico. They built cities and pyramids. The ruins of these cities and pyramids can still be found in Mexico today.

Idea! Velvet rope your kitchen! Before dinner or other mealtime where you are not too rushed, hang a streamer across the kitchen door and before children can enter they must answer the question, "¿Cómo te llamas?".

Week 5: How Old Are You?

Review: Week 4: What is your name?

Vocabulary: ¿Cuántos años tienes?   How old are you?
kwahn-tohs ahn-yohs tee-ehn-ays

Tengo _____ años.   I am _____ years old.
tehng-oh ___ ahn-yohs

cero   zero
say-roh

uno   one
oon-oh

dos   two
dohs

tres   three
trays

cuatro   four
kwah-troh

cinco   five
seen-koh

seis   six
sais

siete   seven
see-yeh-tay

ocho oh-choh	eight
nueve noo-way-bay	nine
diez dee-yays	ten

Grammar note: Translations between languages are not always word for word. In this example, "Tengo nueve años.", literally means, "I have nine years.". We translate always for meaning, and in Spanish we use the words to mean, "I am nine years old."

Cultural Note: In Mexico, people celebrate some fun holidays that we don't celebrate here in the United States. One holiday is El Día de los Muertos or Day of the Dead. On this day, Mexican families remember loved ones who have passed on. Sounds sad? Think again! Families have picnics and feasts and children receive candy shaped like skulls. People tell funny stories about people they loved.

Idea! Buy (or make if you are ambitious) a piñata. This is a fun way to celebrate Mexican culture and also quiz their developing knowledge. Ask each child (en español, of course!) how old they are and when they answer, let them have a whack at the piñata!

Week 6: More Greetings

Review: Week 3, Introductions

Vocabulary: ¿Qué tal?   How's it going?

kay tahl

¡Hasta luego!   See you later!

ahs-tah loo-way-goh

Pronunciation note: Take time to practice your vowel sounds:

a = f<u>a</u>r

e = p<u>e</u>t

i and y = s<u>ee</u>

o = f<u>o</u>r

u = b<u>oo</u>t

Cultural note: Family life is very important in Mexico. Often, three generations live together. Sometimes, extended family like aunts, uncles and cousins live in the same home as well.

Idea! Incorporate these new phrases into your everyday life. "¿Qué tal?" can be used every day while checking to see how the kid's homework is coming along. "¡Hasta luego!" is a great way to say goodbye before leaving for work in the morning.

Week 7: Nice to Meet You!

Review: Week 4: What's your name?

Vocabulary: ¡Mucho gusto!   It's nice to meet you!
moo-choh goos-toh

Igualmente   And the same to you!
ee-gwahl-mehn-tay

Grammar note: This is a phrase that is said at the end of an introduction. Children can tack on, "Mucho gusto" after asking another child their name. "Igualmente" is a useful word in that it can be used after introductions or even simple greetings. For example, just like in English, there are a variety of ways to say, "Have a good day". As your Spanish develops, you can simply reply, "Igualmente" to respond to kind salutations.

Pasa un buen dia.   Igualmente
pah-sah oon bwen dee-yah
Have a good day.

Mucho gusto   Igualmente
moo-cho goos-toh
It's nice to meet you.

Qué tenga un buen día   Igualmente
kay teng-ah oon bwehn dee-yah
Have a good day.

Cuídate.   Igualmente
kwee-dah-tay
Take care (to a friend).

Cultural note: Mexico is a large country with many exciting places to explore. People come from all around the world to enjoy Mexico's beautiful beaches. Mexico contains hot deserts, mountains and even volcanoes! Many people live in tiny, remote villages, but Mexico also contains one of the biggest cities in the world, Mexico City.

Idea! Let your family pretend they have never met. They can make up new names and ages. Let them experiment with the conversational phrases they learned in the last few weeks. Make sure they end their role play conversations with, "¡Mucho gusto!".

Week 8: Review

- REVIEW: ALL BASIC CONVERSATIONAL VOCABULARY.

  o Use dolls or puppets to role play introductions.

  o If you can get up your nerve, introduce yourself to someone in your community who speaks Spanish and encourage your children to do the same. Try to toss out a friendly, "Buenos días". You may feel embarrassed the first time but pleased with yourself afterwards. Remember the point of learning a second language is to speak it!

- LEARN MORE ABOUT MEXICO!

  o Go to a Mexican restaurant.

  o Listen to Mariachi music on YouTube.com.

  o Chocolate originally comes from Mexico. Enjoy una barra de chocolate!

  o Make God's Eyes. These simple crafts can be made with yarn and popsicle sticks and are a traditional Mexican symbol of good luck.

- MAKE YOUR OWN SALSA...or simply buy some and enjoy. This popular condiment is served at nearly every meal in Mexico.

Unit 2:
All About Me

Week 9: Who Am I?

Review: Basic conversation from Week 1-8.

Vocabulary: ¿Quién eres?   Who are you?
                Kee-yen eehr-ays

Soy una chica   I am a girl.
Soy oon-ah chee-ka

Soy un chico.   I am a boy.
Soy oon chee- koh

Soy_____   I am <u>name.</u>

Grammar note: When speaking Spanish, one thing you have to be aware of is gender agreement. Every noun in Spanish is assigned a gender. They are either a male word or a female word. Clue: Many male words end in –o. Many female words end in –a. Every other word that describes that noun or is attached to that noun must match in gender.

Example: chic<u>a</u> = girl   un<u>a</u> chic<u>a</u>= a girl

chic<u>o</u> = boy   un chic<u>o</u> = a boy

As your profiency in Spanish increases, there are more clues and memorization rules to identify the gender of a noun. At this point, simply introduce the concept. Most children find the concept of a "boy word" or a "girl word" humorous. Particularly in light of unusual examples like:

un vestido(m): a dress
una mosca (f): a fly

Cultural note: Spain is a country located on the continent of Europe. Spanish language originated in Spain.

Idea! Give your child the following words: pluma, puerto, banana, libro, mesa, plato. Let them decide if they think each word is male or female.

Week 10: Feelings

Review: Week 3: Introductions

Vocabulary: Estoy triste.   I am sad.
                 Ehs-toy trees-tay

                 Estoy contenta/o   I am happy.
                 Ehs-toy con-tehn-tah (oh)

Grammar note: Note that two possible endings have been included for the adjective contenta. Uses contenta if you are female. Use contento if you are male. This is a great way to practice gender agreement. You can also mix in some previously learned vocabulary:

ESTOY MUY CONTENTA!

Cultural note: The country of Spain has existed for over 500 years! Once upon a time, Spain was filled with many different kingdoms. Today, many of those castles still exist. Spain has more castles than any other country in Europe.

Idea! Come up with funny scenarios to which your child can respond, "¡Estoy contenta!"or "Estoy triste". Examples: We are going for ice cream! We are giving away the TV.

Week 11: What Do I Look Like?

Review: Week 9: Who Am I?

Vocabulary:

Soy	I am...
Soy	
alto/a*	tall
ahl-toh/tah	
bajo/a	short
bah-hoh/ah	
bonito/a	pretty
boh-nee-toh/ah	
guapo/a	handsome
gwah-poh/ah	
grande	big
grahn-day	
pequeño/a	small
peh-kayn-yo/yah	

*Again: Adjectives are typically presented with both the male and female endings. You decide which ending to use based on what you are describing.

Example: La chica es alta. The girl is tall.

                   El chico es alto. The boy is tall.

Grammar note: We use both soy and estoy to mean, "I am". Es and esta are forms of the verbs we use when talking about someone or something else. At a later date you will learn to conjugate all forms of these verbs, but at this early stage just expose yourself and your children to their usage.

44

We use soy or es when we are talking about things that will not change.

Examples:

Soy una chica.= I am a girl.

Soy de los Estados Unidos. = I am from the United States.

Ella es una estudiante. = She is a student.

We use estoy and está when we are talking about something that isn't permanent.

Examples:

Estoy triste. = I am sad.

Estoy contenta= I am happy.

El lápiz está aquí. = The pencil is here. (Right now at this moment it is located here)

Cultural note: The guitar is a very popular musical instrument in Spain. Much of traditional Spanish music features the guitar.

Idea! Use your cell phone to call your house phone. Let your kids chat to one another, greeting each other and describing themselves in Spanish.

Week 12: What Do I Look Like?

Review: Week 11: What Do I Look Like?
Vocabulary:

Tengo el pelo_____.   I have_____ hair.
Tehn-go ehl pay-loh

rubio   blond
roo-bee-yoh

moreno   brown
moh-ray-noh

castaño   red
cahs-tahn-yo

Tengo ojos_____.   I have_____eyes.
Tehn-goh oh-hohs

azules   blue
ah-soo-lays

verdes   green
bayr-days

marrones   brown
mah-roh-nays

Grammar note: Spanish words have to match in gender and also in number. If you are talking about more than one noun, all the describing words attached to it must also show that it is more than one.

Example:

You have <u>one</u> head of hair so we say: Tengo <u>el</u> pel<u>o</u> castaño.

You have <u>two</u> eyes so we say: Tengo <u>los</u> ojo<u>s</u> azule<u>s</u>.

Cultural note: Spain is a big producer of olives. They are one of Spain's most important crops. They are sold whole or to make olive oil.

Idea! Have your children draw a self portrait. They can then use their new vocabulary to describe what they have drawn.

Week 13: What I Like to Do

Review: Weeks 11-12: What Do I Look Like?

Vocabulary:

Me gusta...	I like.....
May goos-tah	
leer	to read
lay-yair	
jugar	to play
hoo-gahr	
nadar	to swim
nah-dahr	

Grammar note: In English verbs are action words (run, walk eat, etc.). In Spanish it is the same, but the infinitive of the word actually includes the qualifier to (to run, to walk, to eat, etc.) Therefore when we add the phrase, Me gusta in front of an infinitive verb, we are making a complete statement.

Cultural note: Many of the world's most famous painters have come from Spain. You can see some their works in a famous Spanish art museum called the Prado. A few of these artists are: El Greco, Velázquez, Goya, Miró, Dalí, and Picasso.

Idea! Have each child pick their own activity they like to do (not listed above). Help them look up the Spanish word online or in a Spanish dictionary and make their own sentence. Suggestions: comer, bailar, dormir, hablar, construir.

Week 14: My Face

Review: Weeks 11 and 12: What Do I Look Like?

Vocabulary:

Toca ...   Touch ...

toh-kah

la nariz   nose

lah nah-rees

los ojos eyes

lohs oh-hohs

la boca   mouth

lah boh-kah

las orejas   ears

lahs oh-ray-hahs

Grammar note: In general, when we refer to the parts of the body, we use the word "the" in Spanish. This differs from English where we say "your". The meaning is exactly the same, but the form is different:

Toca la nariz literally means "touch the nose" but in reality means "touch your nose".

*Did you notice that the article "the" matches the gender and number of each word?

La nariz = the nose

Las orejas = the ears

Cultural note: Spain has a variety of different areas. There are beautiful beaches, high mountains and grassy plains. Spain has beautiful countryside and also cities that are famous all over the world like Madrid, Seville and Barcelona.

Idea! Play a version of "Simon Says" called "Mamá Dice". This is a game you can play anywhere to review vocabulary. "Mamá dice: toca la nariz!". Remember, if Mamá didn't say...you are out!

Week 15: My Body

Review: Week 14: My Face

Vocabulary: la cabeza   head
lah cah-bay-sah

el brazo   arm
ehl brah-soh

el pie   foot
ehl pee-yay

la pierna   arm
lah pee-yehr-nah

la mano   hand
lah mah-noh

Pronunciation note: Remember, z is pronounced like s.

Cultural note: Every July, in the city of Pamplona, there is a "running of the bulls". People run through the streets toward a bullring with wild bulls close behind! Many tourists come to watch.

Idea! Expand on your "Mamá Dice" game to include parts of the body.

Week 16: Review

- REVIEW ALL VOCABULARY FROM THE PAST EIGHT WEEKS.

    o Role play conversations

    o Draw self portraits and describe

    o Point out other people and pretend to be them. How would they describe themselves?

- LEARN MORE ABOUT SPAIN.

    o Make a tortilla española for dinner. This is basically a potato and onion omelette- yum!

    o Go to the supermarket to find Spanish olives or citrus fruits from Valencia.

    o Get books from the library about famous Spanish artists.

    o Go to an instrument store and ask the owner to show you a guitar.

    o Read Ferdinand by Munro Leaf.

- YOUTUBE FLAMENCO DANCERS.

Unit 3:
Welcome to My Home

Week 17: Welcome to My Home

Review: Weeks 9-16
Vocabulary:

⬚Bienvenido a mi casa!   Welcome to my home!

Bee-yehn-beh-nee-doh ah mee cah-sah

Pronunciation note: In Latin America, the v is usually pronounced like an English b.

Cultural note: Central America is the group of countries located between Mexico's southern tip and the northern tip of South America. Honduras is a beautiful country located in Central America.

Idea! Take the plunge! Invite someone over, drum up your courage and welcome them in Spanish. If you feel corny, don't worry. The more you use your Spanish, the more natural it feels.

Week 18: Where Is It?

Review: Week 17: Bienvenido a mi casa.

Vocabulary:

¿Dónde está….. ?	Where is……?
don-day ehs- tah	
el baño	bathroom
ehl bahn-yo	
la cocina	kitchen
lah coh-see-nah	

Grammar note: Remember, all Spanish nouns are masculine or feminine. Is el baño masculine or feminine? How about la cocina?

*Recall that está is the form of "is" that refers to things that are not permanent. We also use está when talking about location.

Cultural note: There are two seasons in Honduras: a rainy season and a dry season. When it rains, the water is so warm you could take a shower in it!

Idea! Practice using "¿Dónde está…?" with words you already know. This is a quick and easy way to practice:

 "¿Dónde está (insert your child's name)?"

 "¿Dónde está la nariz?"

Week 19: Where Is _____?

Review: Week 18: Where is... ?

Vocabulary:

        la mesa table

        lah may-sah

        la silla   chair

        lah see-yah

        la puerta   door

        lah pwayr-tah

        la ventana   window

        lah behn-tah-nah

Pronunciation note: Remember, ll is pronounced like an English y.

Cultural note: Honduras contains a rainforest. Within this rainforest, so many forms of plants and animals live that scientists are still discovering more every day. Many scientists go to Honduras to study in the ways native Honduran plants can be used as medicines.

Idea! Hide a prize (something small, a lollipop, or sticker) in your house. Say; "¿Dónde está la mesa?" for example. Send your child around the house till they find it.

Week 20: Meet My Family (A)

Review: Week 19: Where is it?

Vocabulary:

> Este es mi padre.   This is my father.
>
> Ehs-tay ehs mee pah-dray

> Esta es mi madre.   This is my mother.
>
> Ehs-tay ehs mee mah-dray

Pronunciation note: Está and esta look the same but are two different words. Está puts more emphasis on the second syllable: Eh-STAH. Esta puts more emphasis on the first syllable: EH-stah.

Cultural note: The Mayans were a group of people who lived in Mexico and Central America hundreds of years ago. In Honduras, you can see the ruins of one of their cities at a place called Copan.

Idea! At dinner let your kids have fun presenting their mom or dad.

Week 21: Meet My Family (B)

Review: Week 20: Meet My Family (A)
Vocabulary:

¿Quién es este(a)?	Who is this?
Kee-yehn ehs ehs-tay/ah	
Este es mi hermano.	This is my brother.
Ehs-tay ehs mee air-mah-noh	
Esta es mi hermana.	This is my sister.
Ehs-tah ehs mee air-mahn-ah	

Grammar note: Often we look to see whether a word ends in o or a to decide whether it is masculine or feminine. This is a good rule of thumb but there are exceptions. Este is the masculine form of this and in ends in e.

Cultural note: In Honduras, on September 10, people celebrate a holiday called El Día del Niño (Children's Day). On this day, children receive presents and have parties even though it's not their birthday! Some neighborhoods even hang piñatas in the street!

Idea! Car practice: Have your children take turns "introducing" everyone in the car .

Week 22: Meet My Family (C)

Review: Weeks 20 and 21: Meet My Family (A and B)

Vocabulary:

la abuela	grandmother
lah ah-bwehl-ah	
el abuelo	grandfather
ehl ah-bwehl-oh	
la tía	aunt
lah tee-yah	
el tío	uncle
ehl tee-yoh	
la prima	cousin
lah- pree-mah	
el primo	cousin
ehl pree-moh	

Pronunciation note: Remember to blend the sound on abuela: ah-bweh-lah/

Cultural note: In Honduras, like many Latin American countries, extended families often live together. Cousins often grow up together as close as brothers and sisters.

Idea! Go through your family album and identify members of your family in Spanish.

Week 23: His Name Is_____.

Review: Weeks 20-22: Meet My Family (A,B,C)

Vocabulary:

Tu nombre es_____.   His/her/your name is_____.

Too nohm-bray ehs

Su nombre es_____ .   His/her/your name is_____ .

Soo nohm-bray-ehs

Grammar note: Sometimes the words we use in Spanish change depending upon who we are talking about. There are formal Spanish words, which you would use when addressing an older person, teacher, police officer, anyone in a position of respect. Then there are informal ways of addressing people. We use these words when we are addressing friends, close family or people we are very comfortable with.

Tu is an informal way of saying his or her or your.

Su is a formal way of saying his or her or your.

Cultural note: Hondurans are crazy for coconuts! This tropical fruit is an ingredient in most of their most popular dishes like sopa de caracol, arroz con frijoles, and pan de coco.

Idea! Go around the dinner table and tell the name of the person on the right.

Week 24: Review

- REVIEW VOCABULARY AND CONCEPTS FROM WEEKS 17-23.
  - ○ Now you have the phrases, "Toca…." and "¿Dónde está…?" under your belt. These are two of the quickest ways to do impromptu reviews anywhere! Use them whenever you think of them.
  - ○ Throw an old magazine in your car. When you have some wait time at pick ups or drop offs, ask kids to point to la mesa, la puerta, etc
  - ○ Have a camera phone or digital camera? Let your kids scroll through the pictures as long as they are verbally labeling all the family members they see.

- LEARN MORE ABOUT BEAUTIFUL HONDURAS!
  - ○ Locate Honduras on a map.
  - ○ Crack open a coconut. This requires a little know how but is really fun and memorable.
  - ○ Go to the zoo. Find some animals that live in Honduras.
  - ○ Read about the ancient Mayans.
  - ○ Prepare a baleada. This is a popular Honduran dish consisting of a flour tortilla, refried beans and cheese.

Unit 4:
Useful Information

Week 25: Days of the Week

Review: Review weeks 17-24

Vocabulary:

lunes loo-nays	Monday
martes mahr-tays	Tuesday
miércoles mee-yair-koh-lays	Wednesday
jueves hway-bays	Thursday
viernes bee-yair-nays	Friday
sábado sah-bah-doh	Saturday
domingo doh-ming-goh	Sunday

Grammar note: The days of the week in Spanish are not capitalized as they are in English.

Example: Hoy es lunes. Today is Monday.

Cultural note: Argentina is a large country located on the southeast coast of South America. It is the second biggest country in South America.

Idea! Learning the days of the week is pure rote memory. Make a song out of them to the tune of the Adams Family Theme Song:

"El lunes and el martes,

el miércoles, el jueves,

 el viernes, el sabado

and last el domingo

APOLOGIES TO SONG WRITERS EVERYWHERE...IT'S A STRETCH BUT A SONG WILL HELP THE KIDS REMEMBER.

Week 26: What Day is Today?

Review: Week 25: Days of the Week

Vocabulary:

¿Qué día es hoy?   What day is today?

kay dee-uh ehs oy

Pronunciation note: Remember, h is always silent.

Cultural note: Argentina has three different regions. The warm humid north is called the Gran Chaco. The large central region is called the Pampa. The southern, cold region is called Patagonia. Most people in Argentina live in the Pampa, or central plains. Buenos Aires, Argentina's largest city is located in this region.

Idea! Ask your kids each morning before they start their day, "¿Qué día es hoy?"

Week 27: Amounts

Review: Week 5: How Old Are You?

Vocabulary:

mucho/a	a lot/many
moo-choh/ah	
poco/a	a few
poh-koh/ah	
más	more
mahs	
menos	less
may-nohs	

Grammar note: These four phrases can add more complexity to your growing Spanish vocabulary. They add nuance to simple phrases. Should a waiter in a Spanish restaurant ask, "Would you like more guacamole?" instead of simply responding sí or no, you can reply:

Sí, un poco mas, por favor.

No, tengo mucho, gracias.

Cultural note: Many different kinds of wildlife live in Argentina because the climate is so different. In the warm north there are flamingos and in the cold south there are penguins!

Idea! Use playing card to help kids memorize their numbers. Hold up a card and if the child says the correct number in Spanish, they get to keep the card. Make the joker worth cero and the jack, queen and king worth diez.

Week 28: How Many?

Review: Week 27: Amounts

Vocabulary:

¿Cuántos/as?   How many?

Kwahn-tohs/ahs

Grammar note: Remember gender and number agreement? When you are counting objects, you have to match cuántos or cuántas to the name of the objects you are counting.

Example: Cuántos libros? (How many books?)

Cuántas plumas? (How many pens?)

Cultural note: Argentina's largest city is Buenos Aires. It is world famous for its theaters, museums, libraries and cathedrals.

Idea! Review previous vocabulary through counting. ¿Cuántos chicos? ¿Cuántas sillas?

Week 29: Months

Review: Week 25: Days of the Week

Vocabulary:

enero	January
eh-nair-oh	
febrero	February
feh-brayr-oh	
marzo	March
mahr-soh	
abril	April
ah-breel	
mayo	May
migh-yo	
junio	June
hoo-nee-yo	
julio	July
joo-lee-yo	
agosto	August
uh-gohs-toh	

septiembre	September
sehp-tee-ehm-bray	
octubre	October
ohk-too-bray	
noviembre	November
noh-bee-ehm-bray	
diciembre	December
dee-see-ehm-bray	

Pronunciation note: Remember, j is pronounced like an English h

Cultural Note: Tango is a famous type of music and dance that comes from Argentina.

Idea! With the exception of enero, Spanish months sound similar to their English counterparts. Use this similarity to help your kids memorize them.

Give your children a clue and they have to guess the month you are talking about in English:

Clue: The flowers bloom in mayo. Answer: May

Clue: We fly kites in marzo. Answer: March

Week 30: I Know.....

Review: Week 29: Months of the Year and Week 25: Days of the Week

Vocabulary:

Sé ...   I know...

say

los días de la semana   the days of the week

lohs dee-yahs day lah seh-mah-nah

los meses del año   the months of the year

lohs may-says dehl ahn-yo

Grammar note: If the word de precedes the word el we combine the two into the word del.

We do this with English words like can't or isn't.

Cultural note: Gauchos are famous Argentine cowboys. They lived on the Pampas taming wild horses and gathering cattle. Modern Argentine horsemen are still called gauchos.

Idea! Let your kids brag! Encourage them to tell Grandma, or their teacher, or friend that they know the days of the week and the months of the year. Every time they use their Spanish to communicate (even to brag a little) they are learning more of the language!

Week 31: When Is Your Birthday?

Review: Week 29: Months of the year
Vocabulary:

¿Cuándo es tu cumpleaños?   When is your birthday?

kwahn-doh ehs too coomp-lay-ahn-yohs....

Mi cumpleaño es en ......   My birthday is in.....

mee koomp-lay-ahn-yohs ehs...

Grammar note: Just as there is a formal and informal "you" in Spanish (Usted and Tu) there is a formal and informal your in Spanish. Here we are using the informal tu because most likely you would be asking the birthday of a child or someone you know well.

Cultural note: People in Argentina hold a festival called Carnival. People dress in colorful costumes. Parades full of colorful floats run through the streets. Carnival begins on the Friday before the Christian holiday of Ash Wednesday.

Idea! If your child's birthday is between 1-10 let them try to figure out how they would say the date of their birth: "es seis de diciembre".

If their birthday is a bigger number, help them look up the number and figure it out!

Week 32: Review

- LEARNING ALL THIS USEFUL INFORMATION REQUIRES A LOT OF MEMORIZATION.

    o Use playing cards or preschool counting flashcards to review numbers.

    o Count cars on the road. How many...trucks, red cars, motorcycles, etc.

    o Practice your days of the week song or create your own.

    o Try some fun games and videos available online. I like the games on

    123teachme.com

    and bbc.co.uk/schools/primarylanguages/Spanish

    o Have a group birthday party. Bake cupcakes or another tasty treat. Everyone has to state their birthday in order to get their treat.

- LEARN MORE ABOUT ARGENTINA

    o Google videos of the Tango

    o Look up pictures of stunning Iguazú Falls

    o Some of the largest and oldest fossils have been found in Argentina. Try and find out which dinosaurs were unearthed in Argentina.

- TELL THE ROMANTIC (AND EDITED FOR CHILDREN) STORY OF EVA AND JUAN PERON.

Unit 5:
Mealtimes

Week 33: I'm Hungry

Review: Concepts from Weeks 25-32
Vocabulary:

¿Tienes hambre?   Are you hungry?

tee-yehn-ays ahm-bray

Tengo hambre.   I'm hungry.

tehng-goh ahm-bray

Grammar note: In Spanish, when we answer a question in the negative, the no is often repeated. Example:
¿Tienes hambre?

No. No tengo hambre.

Cultural note: Puerto Rico is a mountainous island famous for its beautiful beaches. People come from all over the world to vacation in Puerto Rico.

Idea! This is one of the easiest conversations to practice because we all have meals every day! Incorporate this simple question into your regular mealtimes.

Week 34: Favorite Foods

Review: Week 33: I'm hungry
Vocabulary:

la hamburguesa hamburger
lah ahm-ber-gay-sah

la manzana   apple
lah mahn-sahn-ah

la torta   cake
lah tohr-tah

el queso   cheese
ehl kay-soh

las galletas   cookies
lahs guy-yeht-tahs

las zanahorias   carrots
lahs sahn-uh-hohr-ee-ahs

Pronunciation note: Remember ll is pronounced like an English y.

Cultural note: Puerto Rican food is a mix of many cultures because so many people have come to live on this beautiful island. Soups and stews are very popular meals. A meal served for a party might be lechón asado- roasted whole pig!

Idea! Brainstorm your own list of favorite foods. Your kids will learn their own favorites quicker if they have to ask for them in Spanish in order to receive them!

Week 35: I Like……

Review: Week 34: Favorite foods

Vocabulary:

¿Te gusta….?	Do you like….?
tay goos-tah	
Me gusta…..	I like….
may goos-tah	

Grammar note: Remember when learning a new language, we translate for meaning, not word for word. Different languages have different ways of phrasing things. If we translated Me gusta literally, it would mean, "It pleases me".

Cultural note: Puerto Rico is a commonwealth of the United States. That means that Puerto Ricans are citizens of the United States but they can't vote in Presidential elections unless they are living in one of the States.

Idea! You can have a lot of fun practicing this concept. Tell the children they are having horrible things for breakfast, lunch, or dinner and innocently ask them, "¿Te gusta?" Remind them to use their emphatic double negative when they reply, "¡No! ¡No me gusta!".

Week 36: I'm Thirsty!

Review: Week 33: I'm hungry!

Vocabulary:

¿Tienes sed?	Are you thirsty?
tee-yehn-ays sehd	
Tengo sed.	I'm thirsty.
tehng-goh sehd	

Grammar note: The phrase, "Tengo sed." literally means "I have thirst". Similarly, "Tengo hambre." means, "I have hunger." This is yet another example of why we translate for meaning, not word for word.

Cultural note: The coqui is a teeny tiny tree frog only one inch long. The coquis begin to sing when the sun goes down. Puerto Ricans love their little lullaby songs and have written many songs and poems about them.

Idea! A hot summer's day is a great time to make a pitcher of lemonade and see who is thirsty. Weather not warm? Try and make some hot cocoa instead!

Week 37: Can I Have......?

Review: Week 34: Favorite foods

Vocabulary:

¿Puedes darme_____, por favor? Can I have_____, please?

pway-days dahr-may pohr fah-bohr

Grammar note: As in English, there are more than one ways to request things in Spanish. Just like in English, it is important to ask politely, adding por favor.

Cultural note: Before the Spaniards discovered the island of Puerto Rico, it was populated by a people known as Taino Indians. The Tainos were a gentle, civilized people who helped the Spaniards settle into their new island home.

Idea! Make snack time practice time! Let your children pick their own afternoon snack and then ask for it – en español-of course!

Week 38: Sit at the Table

Review: Week 37: Can I have...?

Vocabulary:

Siéntate en la mesa.   Sit at the table.

see-yehn-tah-tay ehn lah may-sah

Grammar note: Sometimes in Spanish we attach the pronoun directly to the end of the verb. Here we are saying. "Sit down at the table, you!"

Cultural note: El Dia de Reyes (The Day of the Kings) is a holiday celebrated in Puerto Rico. In the Christmas Story there are three kings, or wise men, who visit the baby Jesus. On La Visperia de Reyes, the night before the Day of the Kings, children cut grass and put it in a box under their bed for the Kings' camels to eat. If the children were good all year, the Three Kings leave a gift!

Idea! Assign a "dinner helper" who gets the rest of the family to the table each night. Pick a different dinner helper every night so each child gets a chance to practice using and listening to this command.

Week 39: Where Is My.....?

Review: Week 38: Sit down at the table.

Vocabulary:

el vaso	cup
ehl bah-soh	
el tenedor	fork
ehl tehn-ah-dohr	
el cuchillo	knife
ehl koo-chee-yoh	
la cuchara	spoon
lah-koo-chahr-ah	
y	and
ee	

Grammar note: Remember what you know about article agreement and plurals. How would you say, "Give me the knives."?

Cultural note: A popular shop in Puerto Rico is called a panadería. A panadería is like a bakery, deli and café all rolled into one. There are different panaderías in different neighborhoods all throughout the island.

Idea! Pair up different items you have previously learned using your new word y. Mama dice with two items instead of one.

Example: Mama dice, "Toca la nariz y la boca".

Week 40: Review

- MEALTIME VOCABULARY IS SOME OF THE EASIEST VOCABULARY TO LEARN. Practice times occur every day so it feels easy and natural to incorporate these words. In addition, children enjoy learning and using the names of their favorite foods.

    o At a restaurant, see if you can translate any items on the menu.

    o Mix your old vocabulary with new. When asked, "¿Cómo estás?" you can respond, "Tengo hambre". You can use the phrase, ¿Dónde está …?" to locate food items on the table.

- LEARN MORE ABOUT PUERTO RICO!

    o Read about famous Puerto Ricans: Roberto Clemente, Marc Anthony, Ricky Martin, Benicio del Toro and Jorge Pasado, to name a few.

    o Teach your kids Puerto Rico's alternate name: Boricua.

- THE MIX OF TAINO, AFRICAN AND SPANISH CULTURES ON PUERTO RICo has resulted in a vivid folklore. Look up some of these colorful tales to retell to your kids- but maybe not at bedtime!

Unit 6:
Getting Ready

Week 41: Wake Up!

Review: Vocabulary and concepts from weeks 32-39.

Vocabulary:

¡Despierta!   Wake up!

dehs-pee-yehr-tah

¡Buenos días, mi(s) hijo/a/os/as! Good morning, my child/children!

Bwehn-ohs dee-yahs mees-ee-hoh/ah/ohs/ahs

Pronunciation note: Hijo/a has a couple tricky sounds to remember. The Spanish h is silent and the Spanish j sounds like an English h. hijo= ee-hoh

Cultural note: Cuba is the largest country in the Carribean Sea. It is located very close to Florida.

Idea! Turn on the daily talk show ¡Despierta America! one morning. The anchors of the show are very animated, you and your children can try and catch words you already know to catch the meaning of each news item.

Week 42: Getting Ready

Review: Week 41: Wake up!

Vocabulary:

Me lavo la cara.	I wash my face.
may lah-boh lah cah-rah	
Me lavo los dientes.	I brush my teeth.
may lah-boh lohs dee-ehn-tays	
Me visto	I get dressed.
may bees-toh	

Grammar: You may remember that when we are writing or speaking about parts of the body we use the articles el or la instead of the pronoun mi. In order to be clear about whose face we are washing, we use a special type of verb called the reflexive. Essentially, we are saying "I wash my face myself". It's a tricky concept, so at this stage just remember to use me lavo in place of lavo when you are talking about washing yourself.

Cultural note: Cuban music is famous all over the world. It is a combination of African music and Spanish music.

Idea! Have your child tell you what he has to do in the morning before he leaves for school or otherwise starts his day.

Week 43: I Want To Wear.....(A)

Review: Week 42: Getting ready
Vocabulary:

Quiero llevar......	I want to wear....
kee-yehr-oh yay-bahr	
la camiseta	tee shirt
lah cah-mee-seh-tah	
los pantalones	pants
lohs pahn-tah-loh-nays	
el vestido	dress
ehl behs-tee-doh	
la falda	skirt
lah fahl-dah	
los pantalones cortos	shorts
lohs pahn-tah-loh-nays	

Grammar note: Remember number agreement. You must match your pronoun or article to your noun.

Examples: Quiero llevar mi camiseta y mis pantalones cortos.

Cultural note: At Cuban schools, all students wear a uniform. Every grade has a different color uniform.

Idea! Before you put your kids to bed, help them pick out their outfits using their Spanish vocabulary.

Week 44: I Want To Wear ...(B)

Review: Week 43: I want to wear....(A)

Vocabulary:

rosa	pink
roh-sah	
roja	red
roh-hah	
azul	blue
ah-sool	
verde	green
bayr-day	
blanco	white
blahn-koh	
negro	black
nay-groh	
naranja	orange
nah-rahn-hah	
amarillo	yellow
ah-mah-ree-yoh	
mojado	purple
moh-hah-doh	

Grammar note: In Spanish, the adjective (describing word) comes after the noun it is describing.

In English we say: I want to wear the green tee shirt.

In Spanish we say: Quiero llevar la camiseta verde.

Cultural note: Many Cuban families only have one child.

Idea! Play I Spy using your new color words. Of course, when we are studying Spanish we don't play I Spy we play Yo Veo Algo…. (I see something…).

Week 45: Where Are Your Shoes?

Review: Week 44: I want to wear...(B).

Vocabulary:

¿Dónde están tus zapatos?   Where are your shoes?

dohn-day ehs-tahn toos sah-pah-tohs

¡Están aquí!   Here they are!

ehs-tahn ah-kee

Grammar note: You already know that ¿Dónde está...? = Where is....?

When we are speaking of more than one item, the verb está changes to están.

This is similar to how we change the word is to the word are when we are looking for more than one item.

Example: Where is your shoe?   (¿Dónde está tu zapato?)

Where are your shoes?   (¿Dónde están tus zapatos?)

Cultural note: Baseball is the national sport of Cuba.

Idea! Hide some everyday items and make the phrase, ¿Dónde están? the start of a treasure hunt!

Week 46: It's Time To Go!

Review: Weeks 2 and 6: ¡Adios! and ¡Hasta luego!

Vocabulary:

> ¡Es hora de ir!   It's time to go!
>
> ehs oh-rah day eer

Pronunciation note: Don't forget, the Spanish h is silent. Hora sounds like oh-rah.

Cultural note: Havana is the capital of Cuba. There are many, many, cars from the 1950's in Havana. People call it a "rolling museum" because looking at the streets is like looking at a street on the 1950's!

Idea! Give each child a turn to sound the morning alarm. Let them announce, ¡Es hora de ir! Maybe it will help get you out of the house on time!

Week 47: Have A Good Day!

Review: Week 46: It's time to go!

Vocabulary:

¡Que tenga un buen día!   Have a nice day!

kay tehng-ah oon bwehn dee-ah

Pronunciaton note: Remember to blend your sounds when putting a b and u together.

Buen = bwen

Cultural note: Plantains are a fruit similar to a banana. In Cuba, plantains are served in many dishes. One way of eating them is to fry them, known as plátanos maduros. Delicious!

Idea! Go to a restaurant or shop you know is owned by someone who speaks Spanish and wish them, " ¡Que tenga un buen día!".

Week 48: Review

- REVIEW ALL THE VOCABULARY AND CONCEPTS FROM THE PAST WEEKS.

    o Incorporate your new vocabulary when getting

      dressed every day.

    o Pretend! Play puppets, paper dolls or Barbies with your kids and use your Spanish vocabulary to get them dressed.

    o Label clothing you see in stores when you are out

      shopping.

- LEARN MORE ABOUT CUBA!

    o Make a Cuban sweet treat. Go online and get a recipe for bunuelos (sweet puffs), plátanos maduros (fried plaintains) or natilla (cuban pudding).

    o Listen to some Cuban music. There are many varieties!

    o Learn to mambo or salsa dance!

- LOOK ON A MAP TO ILLUSTRATE HOW CLOSE CUBA IS TO THE UNITED STATES.

Unit 7:
A Few Odds and Ends

Week 49: Things Around the House

Review: Vocabulary from weeks 41-47
Vocabulary:

la cama	bed
lah cah-mah	
el sofá	sofá
ehl soh-fah	
la lámpara	lamp
lah lahm-pah-rah	
el teléfono	telephone
ehl tehl-eh-fah-noh	
la computadora	computer
lah kohm-poo-tah-doh-rah	

Grammar note: Sometimes there are exceptions to our gender rule guidelines. Look at el sofa. Although the word ends in a it is still considered a masculine word!

Cultural note: In the United States, Latin American people make up 15% of our total population. About 45 million Latin Americans live in the United States.

Idea! Play ¿Caliente o frío? (Hot or Cold?). Play the same way you would play Hot or Cold? But instead of hiding an item, you simply think of one in the room and direct your children toward it by saying caliente or frío. When they find it they have to tell you what it is in Spanish. Then they get a turn!

Week 50: Things in Our World.

Review: Week 21: Who is this?

Vocabulary:

¿Qué es eso?	What is this?
kay ehs ehs-oh	
el autobús	bus
ehl ow-toh-boos	
el coche	car
ehl koh-chay	
el cielo	sky
ehl see-eh-loh	
la calle	street
lah kigh-yay	
las personas	people
las payr-soh-nahs	
el tren	train
ehl trayn	
el río	river
ehl ree-yoh	

la flor   flower

lah flohr

el árbol   tree

ehl ahr-bohl

Grammar note: If you want to say the, you use el or la.

If you want to say a, you use un or una.

Example: Es una flor. = It is a flower.

Es la flor. = It is the flower.

Cultural note: Many of our favorite foods have Spanish origins. Corn chips and salsa are one popular example. Other Americanized dishes of Latin American origin are chicken and rice and black bean soup.

Idea! Use the question, ¿Qué es eso? to practice mixing up you articles and pronouns. Try different ways of answering the same question:

It is my car/ It is the car. Es mi coche/Es el coche.

It is a train/It is the train. Es un tren/Es el tren.

Week 51: Places We Go

Review: Week 50: Things in our world

Vocabulary:

Vamos a .... bah-mohs ah	Let's go to.....
la escuela lah ehs-kway-lah	school
el restaurant ehl rehs-towr-rahn-tay	restaurant
la tienda lah tee-yehn-dah	store
la playa lah pligh-yah	beach
el parque ehl pahr-kay	park
el cine ehl see-nay	movies
el banco ehl bahn-koh	bank

Grammar note: When a goes before el we combine them to form the word al.

Example: Vamos al cine.

Cultural note: The influence of Spanish culture is especially strong in the Southwest USA. Arizona, New Mexico, Nevada, Southern California and Southern Utah are all filled with place names that originated in the Spanish language. Many buildings reflect the Spanish colonial style.

Idea! Make running errands a learning experience. Narrate where you are headed as you run around town and let your kids translate before you get there!

Week 52: Review

- REVIEW YOUR VOCABULARY FROM WEEKS 49-51.

- HAVE A FIESTA! You did it! A year of studying a foreign language is no small feat. Plan a party for you and your children. Incorporate some of the foods and customs you have learned about over the past year. Don't be afraid to mix and match!

- KEEP PRACTICING YOUR SPANISH VOCABULARY. The more you speak, the more you will retain.

- KEEP LEARNING! READ SPANISH LANGUAGE STORYBOOKS. Listen to Spanish songs and music. Hopefully you have embarked on a love affair with this new language. Keep your curiosity piqued and bring your children along for the ride!

Where Do I Go From Here?

Here you are, a year or so later with a good deal of spoken vocabulary in your pocket. What's next? That question can only be answered by you. The key to mastering any language is to continue speaking it. No amount of studying can make you fluent if you don't reach out to others and try to communicate. Continue to make learning Spanish a family affair. You will always have study buddies and you will be giving your children a priceless gift. Utilize the internet to find others who are interested in practicing their Spanish. Join social groups and take daily opportunities to use the Spanish you have already obtained.

For more formal instruction, you can register for inexpensive courses online through any number of companies. There are many companies operating out of Spanish speaking countries that offer lessons through Skype for just a few dollars a lesson. Also available online are courses through the Instituto Cervantes, a nonprofit organization run by the Spanish government. The organization's goal is to promote Spanish language and culture internationally.

Many libraries have audio and computer courses available to lend. Some libraries even offer Spanish/English tutoring classes. This is a great way to meet native Spanish speakers, improve your spoken Spanish, and help someone at the same time.

Another affordable option is to attend local community Spanish courses for adult learners. Most communities offer seasonal enrichment courses, and Beginner's Spanish is very often one of the choices. You may meet other people interested in learning Spanish with whom you can practice.

If you are very goal oriented, or want to receive certification of some sort, you can attend classes at a community college where you live. This will certainly increase your knowledge of written Spanish. Course offerings vary and usually don't extend beyond beginner-intermediate levels. If you want to delve deeper into the language, you can set the long term goal of receiving your DELE (Diploma in Spanish as a Foreign Language). This diploma is granted through the Instituto Cervantes after you work your way through six levels of Spanish instruction and pass an exam. This is a course you take if you are committed to achieving near fluency. It is an internationally recognized certificate you can put on your resume if you are learning Spanish for professional reasons. It is also quite a personal accomplishment!

There are so many free resources available nowadays online that you can easily continue your Spanish language learning on your own time . The next section outlines many free resources you can use to increase your Spanish skills.

Learning Resources

All websites, smart phone applications and podcasts listed below are available for free. Books and music should be available at most local libraries.

INTERNET SITES

Spanishplayground.net: This is a wonderful site containing many fun and educational activities you can use while learning and teaching Spanish. Activities are updated frequently and you can also search for learning resources by category (numbers, days of the week, etc.).

miscositas.com: Curated by an experienced Spanish teacher, this site is a treasure trove of printable materials, links to videos, examples of realia from foreign cultures and teaching ideas. As the site proclaims: It is designed for teaching *and* learning Spanish.

YouTube.com: We all love youtube.com for funny emails but it really is an invaluable teaching resource when you want to learn about or expose your children to different cultures.

googletranslate.com: Hit this site for quick general translations.

spanishdict.com: Go here for accurate translations, definitions and examples of words in context. There are many features of the site to explore, and you can access specific lessons related to what you are currently working on.

123teachme.com/learn_spanish/: You will find a selection of fun, interactive games designed to let children (or adults!) practice basic vocabulary.

Spanishtown.ca/spanishforkids: If you are looking to extend learning beyond the oral/auditory model, there are engaging worksheets here you can print for free.

studyspanish.com: This is a great learning resource for grammar, vocabulary and pronunciation questions. Clear, concise explanations are provided with quizzes to test learning.

livemocha.com: Do you like Facebook? This site is designed to promote communication with language learners all over the world. You can email or chat with members in English or Spanish. Complimentary lessons are available. You can also earn "money" towards fee based lessons by correcting the lessons of English language learners. In addition, great pictures taken by locals of foreign countries all over the world are available for viewing in the "Explore Culture" section.

 bbc.co.uk/schools/primarylanguages/Spanish: This is a terrific site for children. Spanish vocabulary is divided up into topics. Explanations are provided for each topic, and corresponding games are available to reinforce learning.

Mi Vida Loca: Watch this interactive video mystery at bbc.co.uk/languages/Spanish/mividaloca/. Simple Spanish vocabulary is presented through exposure and direct instruction. This is a fun way for an adult to increase their knowledge of beginner's Spanish.

Mango Languages: Lucky for us, our public library provides this online curriculum free of charge. This is a great site for scaffolded, contextual instruction of new terminology. Vocabulary, grammar and pronunciation are all addressed in lessons of increasing complexity. This is a great site and works with many school districts and public libraries. Check out the library near you to see if you can access it from home with your library card.

Muzzy languages: This is a children's language program designed by the BBC. It features animated characters and language presentation through videos, games and lessons. It is a great way to review concepts with little ones. It is also frequently available through your public library.

Destinos: An Introduction to Spanish is an interactive online Spanish course that provides language instruction, listening comprehension practice and cultural instruction. As the website states. Viewers watch a telenovela presented at a slow rate of speech, and peppered with grammar, vocabulary and pronunciation lessons.

APPS

Duolingo: The far and away favorite in our home, this app lets you practice listening, oral, written and reading comprehension within the context of quick, accessible lessons. Our favorite feature: On listening comprehension selections, you can hit a "turtle" to slow down the rate of speech.

MindSnacks Learn Spanish has some really fun games if you want to develop your visual knowledge of the Spanish language. Oral presentation of words is also included with a native accent.

iTranslate is a great feature to keep on your phone. If you want to add to your personal repertoire, or are trying to have small conversations with native speakers, you just type in the word you want to say and it gives you a translation. You can also hit an icon next to the phrase to hear it spoken with proper pronunciation.

ABC Lectura Mágica is an interactive flashcard application. If you want to begin teaching your child to read and write in Spanish there is a built in spelling feature. Most useful is the fact that kids can touch a picture and hear it labeled in Spanish with a native accent. The vocabulary groups are conveniently grouped by category, so you can pick words that complement whatever you are currently learning.

PODCASTS

Listening to podcasts in Spanish is a great way to improve your understanding of spoken language.

Codyscuentos.com is a family favorite. There are many different podcasts to choose from. Classic fairy tales and legends like, "The Tortoise and the Hare" aid in comprehension.

Voicesenespañol.com features a variety of stories, both fictional and nonfictional, that would be of interest to an adult

Coffee break Spanish is another terrific resource for boosting your listening comprehension, and achieving verbal skills. This is a course consisting of eighty short lessons that are aimed at beginners. You can access this free course through iTunes or go to their website at radiolingua.com/shows/coffee-break-spanish.

Audiria.com also has many different podcasts available. The podcasts are organized by difficulty level and topic. After listening, you can access to corresponding text to further your comprehension.

International Tales provides tales from all over the world read by native speakers with perfect accent models. The rate of speech is slow to begin with, and you can slow down the rate of speech even slower with the controls on your smartphone or device.

Notes in Spanish provides enjoyable discussion for adults. It features a married couple, one a native Spanish speaker and one a native English speaker. Children would find the content a bit dry but for an adult their banter is engaging.

BOOKS

The Bilingual Books series, published by Chronicle Books, features classic fairy tales with accompanying text in both Spanish and English. Titles include, Cinderella, Puss in Boots, The Ugly Duckling and many more. Reading aloud to your children from these titles provides great pronunciation practice. The familiar storylines and beautiful illustrations provide meaning clues to help you and your children acquire new vocabulary.

Usborne Books is a publishing company that has created many bright, colorful and interactive Spanish language books for children. Some of their titles are aimed at the youngest children, and contain interactive features like lift-a-flap. Other books are designed to engage older children. Check out their complete selection of titles at myubam.com. Many local libraries carry their books.

Play and Learn Spanish (McGraw-Hill, 2005) by Ana Lomba and Marcela Summerville contains some fun rhymes and short stories you can read aloud to your children and decipher meaning together. Translations are provided and the illustrations are vibrant and engaging.

¡Hablo Español! Creative Activities to Teach Basic Spanish (Incentive Publications, 1995) by Lynn Brisson is a good resource if you want to expose older children to the look of the Spanish written word. This book contains various flashcards and written activities suitable for an elementary age child,

Miriam- Webster's classic Spanish-English, English-Spanish Dictionary is a handy resource to have around the house. Should your conversations with your children lead you to a place that is not covered in this book, you will be able to find most of the language you need in this comprehensive guide.

Affordable Spanish Curriculum:

Spanish for You is a curriculum written by Debbie Annet, a certified classroom teacher. It is designed for use with non-Spanish speakers, and you can work together wwith your child as you both gain fluency. This is a nuts and bolts curriculum, which focuses heavily on verb conjugation. The more verbs you can use, the more sentences you can communicate, so this program gets you and your children speaking the language fast. Also, the verbs presented are kid friendly: drawing, writing, reading, etc.

Celas Maya is an online (as well as brick and mortar) Spanish school based in Guatamala. For real conversation practice, they have tutors with experience working with both children and adults. Their staff is well trained, professional, patient and timely.

Music

Using CD's in the car is a great for listening comprehension.

Songs in Spanish for Children by Elena Paz Travesi is a nice selection of Spanish traditional music.

Fun Spanish for Kids by Beth Manners contains songs and stories easy enough for your youngest children to follow along.

Rockalingua produces a variety of songs designed to teach children Spanish through music. At their website: rockalingua.com, you can access some of their music for free and get a taste of how much fun teaching Spanish through music can be for both you and your child.

Music With Sara is a series of CDs and digital downloads that feature original as well as traditional Spanish language children's music. However, the music and lyrics are so catchy and enjoyable that you may well find yourself listening when no children are around. Highly recommended!

A quién madruga, Dios le ayuda (ah-kee-yehn mah-droo-gah, dee-ohs lay ah-yoo-dah) - He who rises early, God helps

Abuelo/a (ehl ah-bwehl-oh) – Grandfather, Grandmother

Abra (ah-brah) - open

Abril (ah-breel) - April

Adiós (ah-dee-ohs) - Goodbye

Agosto (uh-gohs-toh) - August

Algo es algo; menos es nada (ahl-goh ehs ahl-goh, may-nohs ehs nah-dah) - Something is something; less is nothing.

Alto/A* (ahl-toh/tah) - Tall

Amarillo (ah-mah-ree-yoh) - Yellow

Árbol (ehl ahr-bohl) - Tree

Año (ahn-yo) - Year

Así es la vida (ah-see ehs lah bee-dah) - So is life!

¡Así es! (ah-see ehs) - That's it!

Autobús (ehl ow-toh-boos) - Bus

Ayudame, por favor (ah-yoo-dah-may pohr fah-bohr) - Please help me.

Azules (ah-soo-lays) - Blue

Bajo/A (bah-hoh/ah) - Short

Banco (ehl bahn-koh) - Bank

Baño (ehl bahn-yo) - Bathroom

Brazo (ehl brah-soh) - Arm

Bien (bee-ehn) - Good

¡Bienvenido a mi casa! (Bee-yehn-beh-nee-doh ah mee cah-sah) - Welcome to my home!

Blanco (blahn-koh) - White

Boca (lah boh-kah) - Mouth

Bonito/A (boh-nee-toh/ah) - Pretty

¡Buen trabajo!: (bwehn trah-bah-hoh) - Good job!

Buenas noches (bwehn-ahs-noh-chays) - Good Evening

Buenas tardes (bwehn-ahs-tahr-days) - Good Afternoon

Buenos días (bwehn-ohs-dee-ahs) - Good Morning

¡Buenos días, mi(s) hijo/a/os/as! (Bwehn-ohs dee-yahs mees-ee-hoh/ah/ohs/ahs) - Good morning, my   child/children!

Cabeza (lah cah-bay-sah) - Head

Calle (lah kigh-yay) - Street

Cama (lah cah-mah) - Bed

Camiseta (lah cah-mee-seh-tah) - Tee Shirt

Cara (cah-rah) - Face

Cariño/a (kah-ree-nyoh/ah) - Sweetie

Casa (cah-sah) - Home

Castaño (cahs-tahn-yo) - Red

Cero (say-roh) - Zero

Cierra (see-yair-ah) - close

Cinco (seen-koh) - Five

Cielo (ehl see-eh-loh) - Sky

Cine (ehl see-nay) - Movies

Coche (ehl koh-chay) - Car

Cocina (lah coh-see-nah) - Kitchen

Computadora (lah kohm-poo-tah-doh-rah) - Computer

Cuchara (lah-koo-chahr-ah) – Spoon

Cuchillo (ehl koo-chee-yoh) - Knife

¿ Cómo estás? (koh-moh ehs-tah) - How Are You?

¿ Cómo te llamas? (koh-moh tay-yah-mahs) - What's your name?

Comparte (kohm-pahr-tay) - share

Compórtate bien (kohm-pohr-tah-tay bee-yehn) - behave yourself.

Contenta/O (con-tehn-tah (oh)) - Happy

¿ Cuándo es tu cumpleaños? (kwahn-doh ehs too coomp-lay-ahn-yohs....)
- When is your birthday?"

Cuando hay hambre, no hay mal pan (kwahn-doh eye ahm-bray, no eye
mahl pahn) - When there is hunger, there is no bad bread

¿ Cuántos años tienes? (kwahn-tohs ahn-yohs tee-ehn-ays) - How old are
you?

¿ Cuántos/as? (Kwahn-tohs/ahs) - How many?

Cuatro (kwah-troh) - Four

Cuídate. (kwee-dah-tay) - Take care (to a friend).

Cumpleaño (koomp-lay-ahn-yo) - Birthday

Damelo (dah-may-loh) - give it to me.

Diciembre (dee-see-ehm-bray) - December

Dientes (dee-ehn-tays) - Teeth

Diez (dee-yays) - Ten

Dime otra vez (dee-may oh-trah bays) - Tell me again.

Dimelo (dee-may-loh) - say it to me

Domingo (doh-ming-goh) - Sunday

Donde comen dos, comen tres (dohn-day koh-mehn dohs, koh-mehn trays) - Wherever two people eat, three people eat

¿ Dónde está….. ? (don-day ehs- tah) - Where is……?

¿ Dónde están tus zapatos? (dohn-day ehs-tahn toos sah-pah-tohs) - Where are your shoes?

Donde hay gana, hay maña (dohn-day eye gah-nah, eye mah-nyah) - Where there is the desire there is the ability.

Dos (dohs) - Two

Dulzera/o (dool-sair-ah/oh) - Honey

El mejor escribano echa un borrón (ehl may-hohr ehs-scree-bah=noh eh-chah oon bohr-rohn) - The best scribe makes a blot

El trabajo compartido es mas llevadero (ehl trah-bah-hoh cohm-pahr-tee-doh ehs mahs yay-bah-dayr-oh) - Shared work is more bearable.

Elegios (eh-leh -hee-yohs) - Praise

Enero (eh-nair-oh) - January

¡Es hora de ir! (ehs oh-rah day eer) - It's time to go!

Escucha (ehs-koo-chah) - listen

Escuela (lah ehs-kway-lah) - School

Esta es mi hermana. (Ehs-tah ehs mee air-mahn-ah) - This is my sister

Esta es mi madre. (Ehs-tay ehs mee mah-dray) - This is my mother.

¡Están aquí! (ehs-tahn ah-kee) - Here they are!

Este es mi hermano. (Ehs-tay ehs mee air-mah-noh) - This is my brother.

Este es mi padre. (Ehs-tay ehs mee pah-dray) - This is my father.

Estoy contenta/o (Ehs-toy con-tehn-tah (oh)) - I am happy.

Estoy triste. (Ehs-toy trees-tay) - I am sad.

¡Fantástico!: (fahn-tahs-tee-koh) - Fantastic!

Febrero (feh-brayr-oh) - February

Falda (lah fahl-dah) - Skirt

Flor (lah flohr) - Flower Gracias (grah-see-ahs) - Thanks

Galletas (lahs guy-yeht-tahs) - Cookies

Grande (grahn-day) - Big

Guapo/A (gwah-poh/ah) - Handsome

Hambre (ahm-bray) - Hungry

Hamburguesa (lah ahm-ber-gay-sah) - Hamburger

¡Hasta luego! (ahs-tah loo-way-goh) - See you later!

Hermana (air-mahn-ah) - Sister

Hermano (air-mah-noh) - Brother

Hola (oh-lah) - Hello

Igualmente (ee-gwahl-mehn-tay) - And the same to you!

Imperativos (ihm-payr-ah-tee-bohs) - Commands

Intenta una vez más (In-tehn-tah oon-ah vays mahs) - Try again.

Jueves (hway-bays) - Thursday

Jugar (hoo-gahr) - To Play

Julio (joo-lee-yo) - July

Junio (hoo-nee-yo) - June

Lámpara (lah lahm-pah-rah) - Lamp

Lavo (lah-boh) - Brush

Leer (lay-yair) - To Read

Llamas (yah-mahs) - Name

Lo pasado, pasado está (loh pah-sah-dah, pah-sah-dah ehs-tah) - It past, the past it is

Lo quiero! (loh kee-yair-oh) - I love you!

Los Días De La Semana (lohs dee-yahs day lah seh-mah-nah) - the days of the week

Los Meses Del Año (lohs may-says dehl ahn-yo) - the months of the year

Luego (loo-way-goh) - Later

Lunes (loo-nays) - Monday

Madre (mah-dray) - Mother

Mal (mahl) - Bad

Mano (lah mah-noh) - Hand

Manzana (lah mahn-sahn-ah) - Apple

¡Maravilloso!: (mahr-ah-bee-yoh-soh) - Marvellous!

Marrones (mah-roh-nays) - Brown

Martes (mahr-tays) - Tuesday

Marzo (mahr-soh) - March

Más (mahs) - More

Mayo (migh-yo) - May

Mesa (lah may-sah) - Table

Me gustaría... (may goos-tah-ree-yah) - I would like...

Me lavo la cara. (may lah-boh lah cah-rah) - I wash my face

Me lavo los dientes. (may lah-boh lohs dee-ehn-tays) - I brush my teeth.

Me llamo_____. (may yah-moh) - My name is_____.

Me visto (may bees-toh) - I get dressed.

Menos (may-nohs) - Less

Mi amor (mee ahm-ohr) - My love

Mi angelito/a (mee ahn-hehl-lee-toh/tah) - My angel

Mi Corazon (mee koh-rah-zohn) - My sweetheart

Mi cumpleaño es en ...... (mee koomp-lay-ahn-yohs ehs...) - My birthday is in.....

Mi querida/o (mee kay-ree-dah/oh) - My darling

Mi vida (mee-bee-dah) - my life

Miércoles (mee-yair-koh-lays) - Wednesday

Mojado (moh-hah-doh) - Purple

Muchas (moo-chahs) - Very Much

Mucho gusto (moo-cho goos-toh) - It's nice to meet you.

¡Mucho gusto! (moo-choh goos-toh) - It's nice to meet you!

Muy (moy) - Very

¡Muy bien!: (mooy byehn) - Very good!

Nada (nah-dah) - Welcome

Nadar (nah-dahr) - To Swim

Naranja (nah-rahn-hah) - Orange

Nariz (lah nah-rees) – Nose

Necesito mas (neh-seh-see-toh mahs) - I need more..

Negro (nay-groh) - Black

Nena/e (nay-nah/nay) - cute little girl or boy

No (noh) - No

Noviembre (noh-bee-ehm-bray) - November

Nueve (noo-way-bay) - Nine

Ocho (oh-choh) - Eight

Octubre (ohk-too-bray) - October

Ojos (lohs oh-hohs) - Eyes

Orejas (lahs oh-ray-hahs) - Ears

Oye (oh-yay) - Look out!

Pantalones (lohs pahn-tah-loh-nays) - Pants

Padre (pah-dray) - Father

Para (pah-rah) - stop.

Pasa un buen dia. (pah-sah oon bwen dee-yah) - Have a good day.

Pedidos (peh-dee-dohs) - Requests.

Pequeño/A (peh-kayn-yo/yah) - Small

¡Perfecto! (payr-fehk-toh) - Perfect!

Personas (las payr-soh-nahs) - People

Poco a poco se anda lejos (poh-koh ah poh-koh say ahn-dah lay-hohs) - Little by little one goes far

Poco/A (poh-koh/ah) - A Few

Por Favor (pohr fah-bohr) - Please

¿ Puedes darme_____, por favor? (pway-days dahr-may pohr fah-bohr) - Can I have_____, please?

Puedo tener (pway-doh tehn-air) - Can I have...

Parque (ehl pahr-kay) - Park

Pie (ehl pee-yay) - Foot

Playa (lah pligh-yah) – Beach

Prima/o (lah/ehl- pree-mah/moh) - Cousin (Girl)/(Boy)

Puerta (lah pwayr-tah) - Door

Qué bien!: (kay byehn) - How nice.

¡Qué bonita! (kay-boh-nee-tah) - How pretty!

¿ Qué día es hoy? (kay dee-uh ehs oy) - What day is today?

¿ Qué tal? (kay tahl) - How's it going?

Qué tenga un buen día (kay teng-ah oon bwehn dee-yah) - Have a good day

¡Que tenga un buen día! (kay tehng-ah oon bwehn dee-ah) - Have a nice day!

Queso (ehl kay-soh) - Cheese

¿ Quién eres? (Kee-yen eehr-ays) - Who are you?

¿ Quién es este(a)? (Kee-yehn ehs ehs-tay/ah) - Who is this?

Quiero llevar...... (kee-yehr-oh yay-bahr) - I want to wear....

Quisiera... (kee-see-yair-ah) - I want... (this is a more polite way of saying

"I want")

Repita, por favor (reh-pee-tah pohr fah-bohr) - Repeat, please.

Restaurant (ehl rehs-towr-rahn-tay) - Restaurant

Río (ehl ree-yoh) - River

Rosa (roh-sah) - Pink

Rubio (roo-bee-yoh) - Blond

Sábado (sah-bah-doh) - Saturday

Seis (sais) - Six

Semana (seh-mah-nah) - Week

Septiembre (sehp-tee-ehm-bray) - September

Sí (see) - Yes

Siéntate en la mesa. (see-yehn-tah-tay ehn lah may-sah) - Sit at the table

Sietate (see-yeh-tah-tay) - sit down

Siete (see-yeh-tay) - Seven

La Silla (lah see-yah) - Chair

Sofá (ehl soh-fah) - Sofá

Soy un chico. (Soy oon chee- koh) - I am a boy.

Soy una chica (Soy oon-ah chee-ka) - I am a girl.

Soy_____ (Soy_____) - I am name.

Su nombre es_____ . (Soo nohm-bray-ehs) - His/her/your name is_____ .

Teléfono (ehl tehl-eh-fah-noh) – Telephone

Tenedor (ehl tehn-ah-dohr) - Fork

Ten cuidado (tehn kwee-dah-doh) - Be careful.

Tengo (tehng-goh) - Thirsty

Tengo _____ años. (tehng-oh ___ ahn-yohs) - I am _____ years old.

Tengo el pelo_____. (Tehn-go ehl pay-loh) - I have_____ hair.

Tengo hambre (tehng-goh ahm-bray) - I'm hungry

Tengo ojos_____. (Tehn-goh oh-hohs) - I have_____eyes.

Tengo sed. (tehng-goh sehd) - I'm thirsty.

Tienda (lah tee-yehn-dah) - Store

Tío/a (ehl/lah tee-yoh/ah) – Uncle/aunt

¿ Tienes hambre? (tee-yehn-ays ahm-bray) - Are you hungry?

¿ Tienes sed? (tee-yehn-ays sehd) - Are you thirsty?

Tranquila (trahn-kee-lah) - calm down

Torta (lah tohr-tah) - Cake

Tren (ehl trayn) - Train

Tres (trays) - Three

Triste. (trees-tay) - Sad

Tú (too) - You

Tu nombre es_____. (Too nohm-bray ehs) - His/her/your name is_____.

Un Chico. (oon chee- koh) - Boy

Un mal tiempo, buena cara (oon mahl tee-yehn-poh, bwehn ah cah-rah) - In bad times, put on a good face

Un viaje de muchas millas empieza con un paso (oon bee-yah-hay day moo-chahs mee-yahs ehm-pee-yay-sah cohn oon pah-soh) - A trip of a thousand miles begins with a single step.

Una Chica (oon-ah chee-ka) - Girl

Uno (oon-oh) - One

Vaso (ehl bah-soh) - Cup

Ventana (lah behn-tah-nah) - Window

Vestido (ehl behs-tee-doh) - Dress

Ven Aquí (behn-ah-kee) - come here

Verdes (bayr-days) - Green

Viernes (bee-yair-nays) - Friday

Y (ee) - And

Y sobre todo... (ee-soh-bray-toh-doh) - And most importantly...

Zanahorias (lahs sahn-uh-hohr-ee-ahs) - Carrots

Zapatos (lohs-sah-pah-tohs) - Shoes

About Author

Eileen McAree is a teacher, writer and Spanish language student. She lives in New York with her husband, four kids and their dog, Biscuit.

Did you enjoy 52 Weeks of Family Spanish?

Please share the fun!

Go to the Facebook page, www.facebook.
com/52weeksoffamilyspanish

Give the book a "like" to spread the word! You will also find links to other great Spanish learning activities. I am always on the prowl for fun, easy and effective Spanish activities so the page is updated frequently. Keep checking in!

"Pin" the book on www.pinterest.com and all your followers will get a chance to see the book.

Have a free moment? I am always grateful for reviews on www.amazon.com.

Thanks for reading and keep your eyes open for Color Me Spanish!, due out November 2012.

Made in the USA
Middletown, DE
31 May 2018